The African Mural

'Every race has a soul, and the soul of the race finds expression in its institutions, and to kill these institutions is to kill the soul. No people can profit by and be helped under institutions which are not the outcome of their own character.'
Edward Blyden, 1903.

Paul Changuion
To my wife, Annice, who conceived and co-ordinated this book,
and to my daughter, Sula, and my son, Paul, who shared
this experience with us.

Previous page: Woman, the artist and preserver of values,
images and myths. This page: The geometry of Sotho
architecture is often mirrored in its mural designs.
The step motif emphasizes the harmony between
man and nature.

THE AFRICAN MURAL

Paul Changuion

Text by Tom Matthews and Annice Changuion

NH
NEW
HOLLAND

A typically African equation between art and music — the repetitive,
rough-hewn rectangles are like the rhythmic beats of a drum.

Photographer's acknowledgements

I would like to express my sincerest thanks to: my father, Paul Changuion, for his company during some of the long trips I made in search of murals; Aboo Bakir, for his help in the printing of the photographs; J.C. Laederach, for his help in Lesotho; Peter Malefane of Soweto, who guided me through Lesotho; and Derrick Sherlock, Brian Clouston and the late Stewart Sampson for their help, friendship, enthusiasm and critical judgement.

First published in the UK in 1989 by
New Holland (Publishers) Ltd
37 Connaught Street, London W2 2AZ

Copyright © 1989 in text Tom Matthews and Annice Changuion
Copyright © 1989 in photographs Paul Changuion

ISBN 1 85368 062 1

Editor Bev Bernstone
Designer Neville Poulter
Design assistant Petal Palmer
Cover designer Abdul Amien

Typesetting and reproduction by Unifoto (Pty) Ltd.
Printed and bound in Hong Kong by Leefung-Asco Printers

A detail of monumental flower designs on a Southern Sotho wall — the textures are made by scraping the surface with a knife.

CONTENTS

Preface   11

Introduction   13

Painting and Architecture   21

The Sacred Plant and Other Motifs   41

Doors, Windows and Decorated Interiors   63

Ndebele Mural Painting   87

Southern Sotho Mural Painting   101

Malvel Dani   141

Pictorial locations and map   160

Glossary   163

Bibliography   164

Index   165

A symbol of fertility, the dot is often used as a border.

A Shona dwelling in Zimbabwe. The wide eaves supported by wooden struts protect floral and verbal messages conveying human warmth.

PREFACE

This book is intended for the reader who treasures African art and the people who make it. It is based on authoritative studies in the field which have received both national and international exposure. Its intention is to open the door to a unique form of painting which is undergoing rapid change and, in some regions, is in imminent danger of extinction. There is an urgent need to record and preserve the splendid examples shown on these pages, for their life span is short and their splendour transitory.

That such simple means and humble materials can produce such visual richness, such celebrations of life, is remarkable. Born of the clay of the earth, the colours are at one with the sunlit sky and the surrounding growth, as the earth itself is at one with them. One may travel for miles and see only dwellings of austere and unremarkable plainness, when, unexpectedly, one will come across dwellings, often in clusters, on the walls of which paintings bloom as though some fertile seed had taken root and flowered. We hope that the excitement of these discoveries will be shared by the reader in the pages that follow.

Throughout the book, page numbers precede photograph numbers in pictorial cross-references. For example, 21/3 is page 21, photograph 3. Superior numbers correspond with bibliographical references listed on page 164.

1

INTRODUCTION

The mural art recorded here is the product of a particular type of woman. She is rural, a preserver of traditions. Her life experience is one of continuity rather than change, and with her woman's depth of instinct, she knows the need to keep alive the values and images of her people's past and the myths they embody. Her medium is the mural. She is typically less westernized than her male counterpart, whose contact with urban life is by necessity more frequent and intimate. She is rustic in manner, dress and life style, and the purest and most splendid examples of her art flower, not along highways, but along dusty farm roads and in the open countryside among growing things, among the fields, plants and grasses it so frequently depicts.

It is a domestic art, associated with the dwelling and made by the woman who inhabits it. Both the dwelling and its mural art are so intensely identified with the woman that they are really extensions of herself. In traditional practice the hut is built for and partly by the woman, is known by her name and is a mark of her identity. With its role in creating and preserving life, with its dark, receptive, womb-like interior, it is a symbol of fertility manifested in painted decoration.

The painter does not consider herself a specialist, no matter how renowned her work might be. There is no artist class in her society, but there is recognition that some women are of superior ability and they are called upon to direct the execution of a major community effort. Individuals and specialization, though by no means absent, are not found to the extent that they are in Western society nor have they penetrated as many departments of life.

This woman's art is seasonal. It blooms, wilts and flowers again with the passage of the seasons. It is a fugitive art. Painted on walls of mud, it dies with the temporary surface it adorns. The sun dries it and cracks it, the rain washes it away. Close to the process of nature, it is soon reclaimed by nature. Yet its images are timeless, and in this way constancy and change live side by side.

The fact that practically all of the mural painters and hence

2

1. The Sotho artist is framed in her window, which is surrounded by a stylized flower motif.

2. Enclosed in a ketting motif, the soft images of the veld bloom on the walls of this home.

Backlit by a Zimbabwean sunset, this powerfully sculptured
and painted Venda home contrasts with the mopane bushveld.

many of the most significant creative artists are women is not unique in tribal societies. For instance, among the Californian Indians it is only the women who engage in creative activity, in their case basket weaving. Among the North American Indians generally, weaving and pottery were introduced by women. This is significant in the light of the relationship that exists between tribal weaving and mural painting.

The condition of mural art is bound up with the history of the Bantu-speaking peoples of southern Africa, which is one of a semi-nomadic existence – hence the relative impermanence of the traditional settlement. The Sotho, who are commonly believed to have built more permanent structures, still reveal in the form and layout of the villages their formerly nomadic way of life.

The future of this art, like that of the type of woman who produces it, is tenuous, under the constant threat of progressive urbanization. When she finally vanishes, so will her art. It has no museum life. It is neither transportable nor exportable. Unlike the sculpture of Africa which can retain a portion of its meaning, if only its formal meaning, when removed from its natural environment and placed on a shelf or pedestal in a museum, mural art exists only in relationship with its habitat, and so pays the price of relative obscurity.

The sculpture of the black man in Africa has deeply influenced Western art during this century. There is a vast body of literature dealing with its history, technique and symbolism. Examples exist, more or less well documented, going back hundreds of years. Mural art, the counterpart of man's sculpture, has had no such influence, and even today remains a relatively uncharted field of research.

The written and permanent record of its manifestations is a relatively recent development. It is a 'modern' art in the sense that hardly any examples exist which are more than three or four years old, but it is also ancient and archetypal; works produced today may use conventions similar to those prevalent in Iron Age Europe or in the Middle East thousands of years ago. According to one school of thought, 'the basic variations of African culture which are ancestral to those of today, took place at least 35 000 years ago'.[5]

Among the few records we have of mural painting before the twentieth century, some of the most revealing are those of the missionary, John Campbell. He journeyed to Kurreechane (or Kaditshwêne, not far from present-day Zeerust) and wrote of walls painted with shields, elephants, giraffes and 'other animals' in compositions which seem to be far more elaborate and extensively figural than anything we find today.

In the nineteenth century, the basic motivation of art was thought to be realistic representation, and this was applied as an absolute qualification for all forms of art, ancient and modern. It was believed that art was concerned with the continual perfecting of imitative techniques. Imitation was con-

Woman ('fraus'), plant and seed – the African symbols of fertility – are painted on the undulating surface which is created by a base structure of poles.

1. The step motif and the two-tone colour combination create the effect of dappled light, as though the sun were shining on the wall through moving foliage.
2. The painters invest the simplest geometric forms with unexpected meaning. Note the hubcaps above the door and window.

sidered the mother of art.[1] According to this belief, geometric form was an early, less successful attempt at representation, and was therefore confined to man's early development. This view was consistent with the belief that the two poles of art were on the one hand the ornamental or the purely formal, and on the other the realistic. The religious implications of primitive symbolism had not yet been grasped and an artificial distinction was made between pictorial art and decorative design.

In much African mural painting fertility symbolism is implicit and transcends the merely formal or functional; moreover, attempts at foreshortening and the creation of depth-illusion do occur. It is now generally accepted that the use of geometric form is often symbolic rather than merely ornamental; for instance, the triangle with the apex pointing downward signifying the female. Perhaps many of the designs interpreted today as mere decoration may be traceable to origins having a symbolic significance.

A characteristic common to both primitive art and twentieth-century abstract art is a direct relationship between geometric form and plurality of meaning. A form in which the general is stressed rather than the particular is capable of a variety of interpretations. A tree may become a woman dancing by the addition of legs. Symbols may serve to denote heterogeneous objects; Californian Indians, for example, interpret the same symbol as a lizard's foot, a mountain covered with trees, or an owl's claw. The geometric patterns of the Brazilian Indians represent fish, bats, bees and other animals, although the triangles and diamonds of which they consist bear no apparent relation to these animal forms.[3] Similarly, it has been found that various kinds of animals and plants (the latter is of special interest with regard to African

painting) are represented by figures which show no likeness whatever to their prototypes in nature.[7]

Even the simplest geometric forms can represent plants and flowers (96/1, 108-9). This attitude is due to the fact that, to the primitive artist, there is no inevitable equation between the reality of an object and its outer appearance. The part can stand for the whole; for example animals can be represented by as little as the pattern markings on their skins. Then again, this attitude can be traced back to the curbs imposed by the technical limitations of a medium, such as the basketry designs of the Indians of British Guiana (present-day Guyana), which are explained as animals but are derivatives of geometric forms arising out of the qualities of the material.[3]

The simplest geometric forms can have the most disparate meanings from the course of the sun through the heavens to the flowers and plants of the Ndebele, which have become so schematized and stripped of individual particularities, that they have been interpreted on occasion as lamp-posts. Studies of works in central Africa have shown that a representational intention is discernible even in the seemingly most abstract geometric arrangements.

Eventually even the most talented artists lose track of the different meanings of their images, and many instances can be cited from all over the primitive world where the original meaning of a particular symbol or custom has been lost. Levi-Strauss observed that among most primitive peoples it is very difficult to obtain a moral justification for any custom or institution.[15] They cling tenaciously to ancient customs, though often they are no longer able to account for their original meaning. In a similar way artists may no longer know the significance of their designs, even though they have names for certain types of forms ●

PAINTING AND ARCHITECTURE

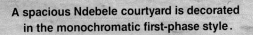

A spacious Ndebele courtyard is decorated
in the monochromatic first-phase style.

1. A young Xhosa stands in the web of shadows cast from the roof structure of her new home.
2. A complex of modules, lying in the untrammelled space of the African veld, segregates generations within the family group and provides a cooking unit apart from the dwelling.

ne tends to associate the traditional dwellings of the black man in Africa with cylindrical, pole- and clay-walled, grass-roofed huts, whereas the range of their forms and materials is rather wider and is still subject to much speculation. The extent of the use of stone, for example, is a question that is by no means settled. The origin of the Zimbabwe and other similar ruins is still a matter of dispute, but a tradition of stone building seems to have been fairly well established. For many years, tribesmen in Lesotho have used stone in the construction of kraals, and in the Northern Free State and Southern Transvaal, the Ghoya and Taung have built corbelled stone beehive huts.

Early descriptions of tribal architecture in central and southern Africa mentioned the use of stone for foundations. The Venda seem to have known something of the use of stone. The rock circles of Engaruka in Tanzania were probably built by Bantu-speaking peoples.[14,15,19] The tendency for mud on grass to replace stone seems, however, to be endemic in traditional African architecture. In about AD 325 King Ezana made reference to the Nobatian towns of straw which replaced the stone structures of the Meriotes whose culture the Noba had supplanted.

During the nineteenth century the missionary, Robert Moffat, described tree dwellings of a type which have long since disappeared: 'My attention was arrested by a beautiful and gigantic tree, standing in a defile leading into an extensive and woody ravine, between a high range of mountains. Seeing some individuals employed on the ground under its shade, and the conical parts of what looked like houses in miniature protruding through its evergreen foliage, I proceeded thither, and found that the tree was inhabited by several families of Kabones, the aborigines of the country. I ascended by the notched trunk, and found to my amazement, no less than seventeen of these aerial abodes, and three others unfinished...'

He noted how 'the ruins of many towns showed signs of immense labour and perseverance; stone fences, averaging

from four to seven feet high, raised apparently without mortar, hammer or lime. Everything was circular, from the inner walls which surrounded each dwelling or family residence, to those which encircled a town.'

'The circular walls (of houses) were generally composed of hard clay, with a small mixture of cow-dung, so well plastered and polished, a refined portion of the former mixed with a kind of ore, that the interior of the house had the appearance of being varnished. The walls and doorways were neatly ornamented with a kind of architraves and cornices. The pillars supporting the roof in the form of pilasters, projecting from the walls, and adorned with flutings and other designs, showed much taste in the architresses. This taste, however, was exercised on fragile materials, for there was nothing in the building like stone, except the foundations.'

The traditional materials for wall-construction in domestic

1. The employment of stone in architecture is a likely origin for painted decoration.
2. The use of various silhouettes is a typical feature of Ndebele architecture; for example, winged portal frames, stepped pediments and crenellations.

architecture are wattle-and-daub, employing the use of poles, laths, grass, reeds and clay. The sun-dried brick is a relatively late development. For many of the inhabitants of sub-Saharan Africa, the archaic medium of grass and reed is used for every conceivable structural need: walls, fences, roofs, chicken coops, even storage bins. As is found in the earliest Nguni dwellings, the roofs are of the beehive type or else are steeply pitched cones, and the walls are low. The

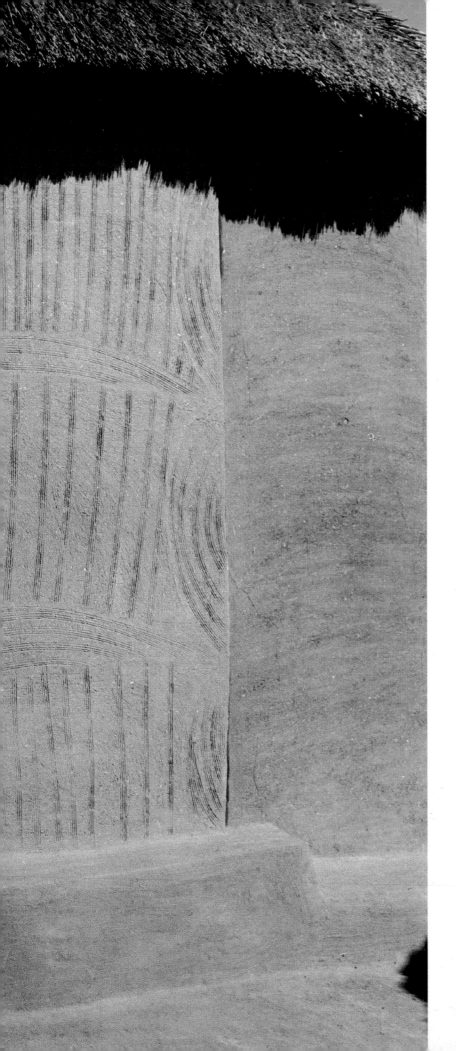

In Lesotho the window is frequently integrated in the design of the facade by means of painted decoration. Of special note is the illusionistic use of dark grey in the shadow areas.

decorative interest is derived purely from the nature of the materials – the regularity or rhythm of the placing of the supporting struts or the contrast of grass on grass.

Among some tribes the roof is thatched in two layers: an underlayer of fine grass which can be packed closely to seal the interior from leakage and a overlayer of coarse, strong, fibrous grass which prevents weathering. Sometimes the underside of the roof-overlap is reinforced with a partial layer. In the construction of the wall, the wattle-and-daub technique is used. It entails planting a skeleton of strong vertical supports in the ground, usually about a metre apart. The next step is to make a grid-pattern of more slender horizontal sticks, which are bound to the uprights, extending to the roof-line by strips of hide, roots, strong grass or, more recently, wire. Sometimes the horizontal pieces may be interwoven with uprights. After these have been bound in place, a further series of slender uprights is placed between the main supports, often no more than an inch or two apart, and these are again bound into

1

place, or sometimes intertwined. The final effect is a kind of primitive weaving, with many uprights and few horizontal supports.

Then the mud (*udaka*) is applied, mixed with cattle dung and sometimes with clay or grass for strength. Usually, two layers of the mixture are applied, one from the inside and one from the outside. The plaster does not necessarily cover the entire skeleton. Vertical members often remain uncovered as a visible expression of the structure. Finally, the wall is plastered with a thin layer of the mixture. If it is too wet, the excessive loss of moisture can cause the plaster to crack, but it must be damp enough to work a series of rhythmically repetitive motions of the hand. The clay assumes a pattern of repeating segments whose radius is about a metre, or the distance that the outstretched arm can comfortably travel over the surface of the wall, producing a wavy relief-pattern that is widely used throughout Africa as far north as the Hausa communities of northern Nigeria. Lacking mechanical aids for obtaining an even surface, the tribal builder imparts his walls with a fine feeling for texture and a subtle modulation of planes which catch the light and impart a strongly tactile and sculptural quality to the surface. The usual plastering proce-

dure is to work in vertical panels, completing one section before moving on to the next. The result is a repetitive tree-like motif which is decorative of its own accord, and after the rain has washed the paint off the hut, these mud patterns remain as the sole means of decoration.

More important than this decorative aspect, however, is the symbolic and architectonic aspects: these patterns at once signify man's desire for identification with nature, and at the same time reassert the skeleton of the building and acknowledge the basic constructive material of wood. The uprights represent trunks of trees, very often corresponding to the structural uprights which they actually cover. The 'branches' are formed by the arc-like motions of the hand, always keeping within the bounds of the vertical panel. The tree motif can vary. Sometimes it is formalized, a simple succession of horizontal arcs between the vertical divisions. Then again it can be treated more poetically, swelling from the wall like a plant in low relief. In time the paint may peel partially off the wall and the plant form will emerge again as the combined work of man and nature. The use of the tree motif exemplifies what one would call functional decoration. Additional ornaments complement this basic motif. Often flower-

1. Close harmonies of geometric design are used to articulate and give interest to large, plain expanses of wall.
2. In Ndebele mural art the rich colours and intricate design are reminiscent of inlaid work or Oriental carpets.

2

patterns on either side of the door continue the rhythms of the plaster decoration.

Among the Southern Sotho, sun-dried brick is used as a simpler and more economical variation of baked brick and mortar construction, and is often acknowledged in the painted decoration (65/2). Sometimes the bricks are cast in simple moulds, sometimes shaped by hand. This type of wall is usually given a final plaster coat on both interior and exterior. The rectilinear dwelling, in contrast to the circular, is frequently found among the Southern Sotho, and in the vicinity of small towns is the only type used. Generally people of the interior used perpendicular walls at an earlier date than did their coastal counterparts.

Both men and women take part in building, each performing their respective tasks. Often women cut grass, thatch and make the floor. When necessary, they also plaster the hut. The men do the work that is heavier but does not take as long to do, such as cutting and fixing the wooden framework and thatching. The women weave the smaller twigs into the framework and plaster them over with mud, and make the hut's floor of liquid cow dung, sometimes mixed with ant heap and ox blood. The ant heap has strong binding qualities, and seeds do not readily germinate in it. The ox blood also has adhesive qualities and adds a glutinous sheen and colour. The decoration of the walls is essentially a village art, made for the enjoyment of all, and is very often a collective activity. Several people can take part but usually under the guidance of the most reputable painter in the community.

Materials and Techniques

The tools of painting are as simple as the media: fingers, hands, rags, toothbrushes (91/2), brushes made from feathers as used by the Bushmen, and occasionally trowels. The parallel ridges of the Sotho *litema* patterns are often made by drawing a fork across the wall surface. Cloths dipped in paint are used to cover large areas of wall space, smaller cloths for less extensive areas. Fine detail is added by using brushes made from whatever materials are available.

The medium must not be too watery, but should be thick enough to achieve covering power and to avoid dripping. When the design is blocked out in large areas, however, the painter often begins at the top and works gradually downward, so that any dripping is eliminated in the actual execution. Simple masking techniques are sometimes used to achieve the typical hard-edge juxtaposition of flat colour areas. The Sotho use cardboard stencils to repeat patterns (122/2). Paints are made by mixing water with powdered colours which may be obtained from rock or clay found locally or which may be shop bought. Designs sometimes combine colours from clay deposits with those distempers which have been purchased.

The mural painter 'feels' her design, rythmically sweeping her arms across the surface of the wall to create patterns or pressing her fingers in the damp clay to make a stippled background in which to set stones. With a large trowel she may sculpt large areas the length of her body, following the form of a plant nearby. Unconsciously she may repeat a pattern with which she is familiar, whether in nature or on a woven commercial blanket.

Sods of earth in the spaces of the underlying structure may show through the final plastering which is usually achieved by means of a home-made trowel. The skeleton is usually covered with layers of mud plaster, often built up over a few years, and subtle modulations of planes may catch the light, imparting a sculptural quality to the surface.

Colours

The African dwelling is essentially in harmony with its surroundings. It rises from the ground like a plant on a rock. It is rooted in the soil and decorated with the colours of the earth. This feeling for the natural ground is seldom submerged even in the most highly coloured paintings.

Earthy colours are often chosen in spite of opportunities to use modern synthetic colours. The most frequently used synthetic colour is washing blue. While red and yellow oxides are readily obtainable from the soil, the addition of this blue virtually provides them with the third primary colour of their spectrum, and its use accounts for the highly chromatic effect that is evident whenever the colours are used together.

Green, used by the Ndebele more frequently than by other peoples, was originally obtained from mineral deposits. It is interesting to note that in the Xhosa language there is only one word for blue and green. If they have to specify which of the two it is, then they describe it either as the colour of the sky or the colour of the trees. (In Fanagalo, the lingua franca of the mining industry, a green traffic light is identified as the 'blue' light.)

While water is usually the only medium mixed with paint, the Ndebele add a little soft maize meal to give body to the whites. Among the Fingo, salt is often added to the white to improve its adherence. The choice of colour matter varies from district to district. Sometimes people walk for miles to obtain a particular colour from a clay deposit.

The people are familiar with the materials from their earliest years. The training of a painter consists in watching the mother, and collecting pigments. There is hardly any suggestion of teaching or instruction in a Western sense.[7] At most a few directions are given now and then, but generally the pupil learns by watching and imitating. To the African, art is simply one of the functions of a human being.

Mural Decoration and Architecture

Mural painting gives significance to the basic architectural features. Even on small huts, there is a monumentality of conception and an instinctive preservation of the surface of the

An element of space-transition, the screen wall separates one courtyard from another.

This splendid example of Ndebele architecture shows the unpainted kitchen area separated by a courtyard from the highly decorated living quarters.

1

wall. The painted decoration emphasizes the structure of the hut, sometimes to the point of being a pictorial re-creation of the method of construction. It turns the most modest door or window into a monumental feature. The sense of scale is not realistic, but decorative and emotional. Huge shapes are frequently used which cover the whole height or breadth of the wall (100-1). Large simple triangular areas may grow upwards and form a dado of leaf-like forms (19/2).

The mural painter uses the most basic and ancient devices of architectural painting: painted dados, window borders, cornices, and ornamental entrances. Sometimes the motifs are concentrated on the focal points of the main façade, the doors and windows. With the Ndebele, however, the emphasis is more overall, and each wall has its own focus within the design itself (28-9/1). Doors and windows have little of the inevitability of relationship with decoration one finds in other mural art. Also Ndebele painting tends to proliferation rather than to sparseness.

It seems likely that the earliest representations of plants on the exteriors of dwellings were always meant as enrichments to the entrance surrounds, and the practice of confining the decoration to door and window areas derives in many instances from the religious significance of the opening. Door decoration is sometimes derived from ritual markings above entrances. In the Qebe area of the Transkei, for instance, part of the healing ritual entails the witchdocter's painting a cross above each threshold in the dwelling complex.[4]

The significance attached to the painted entrance is not, however, always religious or ritualistic. It can also be an expression of structure. Apertures are structually weak points in the wall and are liable to frequent cracking. Consequently, they are the areas that are repaired most often and the final painting often follows lines that have already been established by the repair coat of plaster.

Painted plant forms establish continuity between nature and the man-made environment. Just as Egyptian glazed hippopotamuses from the tombs of the Middle Kingdom are decorated with the swamp vegation in which they live, so the tribal dwelling is decorated with the surrounding growth and is brought into accord with nature. Nature is brought into the interior itself, where the forms depicted are essentially the same as those on the exterior, but can be smaller, more intimate, and more delicate in scale.

A general feature in African mural art is that painting gives scale to architecture and helps clarify the composition of architectural forms that go to make up the living complex. Wall strength is emphasized by a continual echoing of the two basic directions of architecture, the vertical and the horizontal (4-5). Diagonals tend to be inclined at an angle of 45 degrees. Painted form is incorporated with architectural form, so that flower and leaf designs become reduced to geometric motifs; segmented or triangular pediments are placed above entrances, windows, or at the gable-ends of pitched roofs (28-9/1) and are decorated with house or plant designs. The nature of

the wall is asserted with motifs based on elements of building construction. Brick patterns (67/2) or patterns reminiscent of wood and grass construction are often used.

On the main façades of Ndebele dwellings, there is a tendency to break up large areas into smaller units. The decoration can become intense, overwhelming the architectural structure which is then revealed primarily, not in terms of three-dimensional masses, but as juxtaposed areas of colour or pattern. Clarity is maintained, however, by the use of compositional devices found in mural painting throughout the ages: symmetry of composition, formalization of motifs and recognition of the wall surface as part of the design.

Symmetry

Symmetry is one of the most basic features of African mural art. Compositional schemes are often bilaterally symmetrical on either side of a central axis, as are the individual forms within the composition (70-1, 42/1). One of the reasons for this is that the painting functions as an extension of human action, and echoes the structure of the body. A painter, when drawing on the ground in explanation or preparation for mural

painting, often draws with both hands. She begins at the top of an imaginary vertical, and the resultant forms on either side of this are simultaneously realized and are mirror-images of each other.

Movement of the arms and hands are physiologically determined. The right and left are apt to move symmetrically, and the motions of the arms are often performed rhythmically. In this way, gesture, dance and language pass in a fleeting moment but in painting they are given a greater permanence.

This bilateral symmetry has the vertical as its central element of organization. Its presence presupposes the right-angle, the basic element of all architectonic thought, and by consequence it presupposes the horizontal. African mural

1. The doorways of this homestead are darkened by means of painted shadows.
2. In this case the doors and windows are highlighted, not by colour, but by subtle low-relief.

painting is related to this principle of bilateral symmetry; even when the lines vary from the vertical and horizontal they are governed by them: angles of approximately 45 degrees are prevalent, and practically every straight line which varies from the two main directions is coupled with either a vertical or a horizontal.

In addition to bilateral symmetry, we can define two other types: shifting and rotational symmetry. By far the oldest type, the former arises from the horizontal repetition of a single motif (54-5). Rotational symmetry, on the other hand, comes about when a motif turns through a certain angle

before repeating itself (50-1, 144/1). It too appeared earlier than bilateral symmetry and was used as early as the fourth millennium BC. [21]

Two-dimensionality

The great advantage of mud architecture is its plasticity, yet the Ndebele tend to reduce it to an architecture of silhouettes. Two-dimensional effects are found everywhere. To overcome the limited means the builder has at his disposal, emphasis is laid on a variety of silhouettes by means of pediments, crenellations, finials, free-standing pillars and lintelled entrance gateways.

Pediment decorations add strength to the design and affect the transition from rectangular wall surface to gable (28-9/1) or pass the visual thrust diagonally down the wall. When a fully three-dimensional form is used, like the sphere of a finial (99), it is because it presents a circular silhouette from any angle, rather than because it is a projection in depth. Because of this two-dimensionality, one's progress from the exterior, through the portal of the courtyard, and finally through the portal of the interior itself is a progress through a series of screens which are analogous to stage-props in the theatre (31). These screens each mark a transition from one environmental situation to another: from the light-filled exterior to the more human space of the courtyard, and finally into the cool darkness of the interior (84-5/1). These divisions reach their greatest degree of formalization among the Ndebele, who use special terms to refer to the entrance of the courtyard, (*esangweni*) and the entrance to the house, (*emnyango*).

Darkness and Expression

We know that the Egyptians capitalized on the qualities of crepuscular light in their temples and houses. In Zoser's entrance-hall at Sakkara, the world's first monumental, stone-built interior, the windows of the side wall consisted of small slits so that only a small amount of light could penetrate. In Chephren's three-aisled valley temple, the only temple from the Fourth Dynasty whose lighting can be securely established, the sun's rays also enter through narrow horizontal slits in the ceiling.

In prehistory, this love of darkness that is strong in early cultures amounted virtually to a cult. The Magdalenian hunters placed their most sacred images in the deepest part of the cavern. Simple huts with their smoke-blackened entrances, flames gleaming from the darkness of the interior, the narrowness of the doorway often emphasized by the flanking areas of painted white, all remind one that man's first gathering-place was little more than some narrow aperture in a face of rock (see the 'keyhole' entrance, 35/2) ●

1

1. A rare example of the ancestral guardian figure.
2. The living descendent looks down upon the figure of one of his ancestors.

A recurrent African symbol expressing a wider and deeper view of nature – a panoramic plant grows from a heart-shaped tuber.

THE SACRED PLANT AND OTHER MOTIFS

Habitat and Ritual

An examination of the style, meaning and links with the past in mural art reveals a religious basis: in animism and the worship of trees and plants; and in fertility cults, discernible in the recurrent symbols of plant and seed. As man began to develop ideas about gods and spirits he connected many of these ideas with plants - for if a plant could kill, intoxicate or soothe, it must have an inner power.[12] This intimate relationship between plant and human is in fact no more than an all-pervading philosophy which considers all phenomena to be interdependent, linked in a chain of vital forces.

In various parts of Africa ancestors were often venerated in tree form.[6] Today certain forests are still considered sacred. In many traditional societies in southern Africa, a special link exists between the fertility of plants and humans; this is evident, for example, in the ceremonial use of semen and parts of sexual organs to ensure the fertility of grain.

Fertility is the gift of woman, and among agricultural peoples its symbol is the plant. As we have seen, mural painting is essentially a woman's art, and its study necessitates an understanding of the traditional place of the woman in society,

and perhaps even more importantly, the nature of womanhood in its concern with fertility and growth.

It is the woman who tends the fields, and whose being is intimately bound up with growth, fruitfulness and reproduction of crops. Fertility is particularly valued in agricultural societies where life depends on the earth's fructifying power, and the fertility of the crop is the symbol of the fruitfulness of the woman.[19] These are some of the reasons why in southern Africa, and perhaps more specifically among the Nguni and Sotho people, the depiction of the plant is largely the prerogative of the female.

In African mural decoration, plant forms have ritualistic implications even if only through the woman making her mark of possession on the dwelling and identifying it as a product of her life experience. Something that the individual has touched or handled becomes imbued with a portion of her personality.

As a shelter, the hut is intimately bound up with human survival, existence and death. Consequently the functions of the dwelling place have always been enshrouded in ritual: among some tribes a married woman who has not yet conceived her first child may not approach her husband's hut, indeed any hut in the kraal, from the front. Wherever she may be coming from, she must pass round behind the huts and

1

1. In the tradition of the Bushmen and other African artists, the plant takes on an anthropomorphic form, complete with trunk, head and extended arms.
2. This deaf girl painted many dwellings in the complex, including this one depicting a plant and vase.

come to the front from thence. Also, the daughter-in-law may not smear the walls or floor of the man's side of the dwelling. At the end of the confinement period the mother has to clean the hut and freshly smear the walls and floor with cow-dung.

Many rituals seem to focus on the entrance to the hut or village. To protect Lobedu villages, the gateposts were made from a special wood, and were smeared with medicines on the day they were erected.[13] Among the Ndebele, symbolic

emphasis is often given to doorways. Guardian figures may be placed at the entrance of the courtyard or within its confines (38-9). The dwelling is imbued with strongly sexual connotations which is evident in the compulsory ritual intercourse that must take place in the hut between husband and wife before setting up house.

From these observations it may be seen that the dwelling is integrated with a system of ritual which encompasses prac-

2

1, 2 and 3. Found in ancient art throughout the world, the plant and mound, and its derivative, the plant and vase.

tically all aspects of everyday life. Ritual becomes the most binding factor in life, touching almost every facet thereof.

Painting and Geometry

Like so much Black art, wall painting is submitted to rhythmic formalization. Its tendency to what we would call abstraction is partly explained by the fact that it is orientated rythmically rather than visually. Forms are abstracted from the visual world in a way that has much of its inspiration in music and dance. The rough-hewn rectangles that are found frequently in wall painting can be likened to the rhythms of a drum beat (4-5). Its forms and colours are limited to those which make for harmony rather than contrast.

Geometry has always been the most basic symbol of man's control over his environment. To geometricize nature is to

The artist stands modestly beside her simple but beautiful creation produced from the natural colours of the earth.

order it, to submit to schematization. On the other hand, the organic symbolizes nature as mysterious and uncontrollable – not that mural painting rejects the organic principle in nature, but rather it submits it to a primeval, rough-hewn geometry and produces images that are often reminiscent of elementary cultivating implements. It is generally true that traditional African artists unconsciously geometricize their delineation of objects – they tend towards variations on circular or rectilinear forms.

Plant and Woman

As fertility symbols, the geometric plant and flower forms of African painting are invested with human connotations. A tree form may be painted with a tenuous verticality that is anthropomorphic and may be given arms, legs or a head (42/1). Plant forms were used as anthropomorphic images by the Bushmen and by the African artists as far north as Dahomey (present-day Benin).

In Europe there are many beliefs connected with man-plants, most strikingly exemplified perhaps in depictions of the mandrake. Even in later, more accurate botanical drawings, such as those of Pietro Andrea Mattioli, the roots of the plant resemble the trunk and legs of a man or woman.[12]

The geometric forms of the Ndebele, it would seem, may also incorporate symbols of anthropomorphized sexuality. Prehistoric man often symbolized the female by a representation of the vulva alone as a triangle with the apex pointing downward and in Egyptian hieroglyphic script the puedenda of the female were regularly used for the word 'woman'.[18] Containers, especially cups, seem to have significance as female symbols. Earlier we noted how the dwelling may be thought of as female in gender, and the interior is considered metaphorically as a womb. It is not uncommon to find doors in which the metaphor is extended by surrounding it with softly vulvate or foliate forms.

At any rate, the plant-woman equation remains the basis of the most widely used motif in mural painting. In their myriad shapes – formal plants, flowers in vases (45/2/3), flowers with their roots exposed (46-7), plants surrounded by seed-dots which are regarded as symbols of human fertility (17/3), foliate forms so abstracted that a careful tracing of the

1. The dwelling grows from the ground like a plant and is at one with nature.
2. The dancing figures adorning this batchelor's hut were painted by the deaf girl shown on page 43.

lineage of the design must be made before they can be identified (108 - 9) – realistic or geometric, plants are the leitmotivs of African mural art.

Configuration of Dots

In 17/3 the connection between plant and woman is made explicit by a pictorial juxtaposition of a plant surrounded with seeds and the word 'fraus', a derivation of the Germanic term for 'wife'. These configurations of dots or seeds are one of humanity's most ancient images.

A dot is a version of a circle, and the circle has always been equated with the sun and fertility. The Egyptians used it as a symbol of fruitfulness in agriculture,[8] and in African art circles are often specifically related to the fertility symbol of seeds and, by extension, of woman. Examples have been found in African mural painting where rows of dots of the type

1

2

Earth colours are given resonance by the vivid blue
African sky — in this case emphasized by the cerulean
hue of the door.

1

1. Rivers in
mountainous terrain.
2. *Isikwens* is a term
used to denote
chevron patterns and
all curved variations of
these forms.

seen in 17/3 signify sowing and hence the growth of plants. We have noted how traditionally agriculture was the prerogative of the female and in 17/3 the equation between the fertility of seeds and woman is alluded to on several levels. Firstly, the row of dots along the dado has been sown in a line, as though the artist were following a ploughed furrow, and has been juxtaposed with a version of the word 'woman'. Secondly, other images signifying female presence here are the flowers, surrounded by fertility dots.

Water

To the primitive agriculturist, water must necessarily occupy a prime position in the hierarchy of fertility. The Egyptians thought of it as the elixir of life and it was also considered essential to the sustenance of life after death. In cases where it is rendered in terms of more than colour alone, the usual convention is a series of parallel chevron patterns.

The Ndebele often indicate water by means of a similar parallel arrangement of diagonals (92-3), whilst Nguni painters may use a single succession of chevrons (54-5) to denote either water or rocky or mountainous ground. This association is due partly to the appearance of the silhouette of a chevron pattern, and partly to the circuitous course that must be taken in traversing such terrain; to many it is a purely decorative device, the original significance of which has been forgotten.

A river is depicted as a band of chevrons or scallops (54-5), many rivers flowing over mountainous terrain as a lateral succession of diamonds interlocking over two registers (53/2).[4] Xhosa painters speak of these chevron patterns and zigzags as *isikwens*, but also use the term to describe all of the curved variations of these forms – the regular undulatory pattern (52/1), which often runs within parallel lines, and all forms of scalloping. The *isikwens* pattern may also be used as a baseline to denote rocky ground out of which plants may grow. All are among the oldest decorative motifs.

2

A single succession of undulations
or chevrons may denote either
water or rocky, uneven ground.

1. The furrow and the plough.
2. A symphony of textures.

The Step Motif

It may be considered as a basic tenet of primal cultures that no single element of a culture exists without gaining at least a degree of its identity by its contrast or correspondence with other parts. The world of forces is held together like a spider's web. To the tribal mind, man is both against and in harmony with nature. This is a duality that finds its most elementary expression in the need for survival. The habitat, therefore, incorporates this duality on both a constructive and an expressive level, and reveals it in a tension of opposites between the organic and geometric; the first is an admission of the omnipotence of nature, the second an attempt to order it according to the most powerful means for order possessed by man, his intellect. All tribal architecture acknowledges this duality. It leads to two elementary decorative motifs, the tree form of the plastering technique symbolizing the organic and the step pattern which represents man's attempt to control the organic.

In its simplest form the step pattern is an elongated rectangle in the horizontal position, with each of its corners truncated into ascending or descending successions of right-angled steps. This is a form which reiterates the necessary harmony between man, represented by the vertical element, and nature, the horizontal.

Like the chevron or scallop, the step pattern can have many meanings. It may literally represent steps; on the other hand, if two pyramidal step patterns are placed in a vertical mirror-image relationship as a lozenge shape, they may represent foliate motifs (see cover picture). Among the Sotho, step patterns are used as cornice motifs usually in conjunction with chevrons and plates. The Ndebele use a bilaterally symmetrical pyramid of steps which may represent a dwelling, especially if an arched entrance is shown (92-3).

The Tree and Mound

The image of the tree and mound is found in ancient art throughout the world and is widespread in African mural painting. It may be that the presence of the motif is due to foreign trade, notably of pottery. Pottery is easy to transport and may well have reached southern Africa from archaic civilizations like those of Sumeria, Phoenicia or Egypt. We know that in Zimbabwe remains of Phoenician handicraft have been discovered, and the dispersion of the influences southward would seem quite natural.[17] In support of this theory we see that the mound in southern African mural art sometimes takes on a rectangular form (73/1) similar to that of the relatively proximate Near East.

If these similarities are not the result of actual contact in the past, they could be due to the power of the collective unconscious, archetypal emanations of that part of the psyche which retains and transmits the common psychological inheritance of mankind. Corresponding examples can be cited from Akkadian, Scandinavian, Assyrian, Egyptian, and Mesopotamian art. The basic theme of the mound may be transmuted to become a mountain, root system, embryo, womb or vase — some source from which the flower, tree, plant or column grows towards a symbol that could be either seedlike, stellar,

2

1. Low-relief, sculptured plant forms surround the doorway of this Xhosa home.
2. The step motifs used by the Xhosas show clearly on the walls of these huts scattered among the hills of the Transkei.

lunar or solar. It is a symbol of renewal and transcendence, perhaps primarily of contact between man and the cosmos.

The writings of antiquity contain many references to the contact between the peoples of the ancient Near East and the Negroid states to the south. Not that there is any real evidence in the culture of the Bantu-speaking peoples of direct Egyptian, Phoenician or Mesopotamian influence, yet African mural decoration shows features strikingly similar to those prevalent in the Iron Age and the ancient Near East: for example, two-dimensionality of form, severe rectilinearity of composition, and the geometric abstraction of the motifs depicted.

The evolution of the tree and mound theme would seem to follow a sequence from the organic and readily identifiable to the geometrically cryptic, and all stages of this evolution are still to be found in mural art. In 45/2/3 it is in its elementary form in a type of design that was widespread in early civilizations. The mound is a triangular base, the tree invades the 'sky' of the wall space. The fully evolved geometric variations of this can be seen on pages 108-9. The actual window has become the centre of a plant with its stem rising from a stepped mound. In 73/1 the mound has become a rectangular base, while the tree has become a symmetrical cruciform. Its base is not so much a mound as a flower pot, and indeed the flower in a pot (16/2) is a widespread variation on the tree-mound theme. In other variations the mound has become a root, a tuber from which a flower sprouts, and on pages 46-7 the representation is specific enough to be identifiable as a flowering sweet-potato, while other flowers and roots spread across the wall as minor variations of the main theme.

1

Hands

Among the earliest pictorial images ever used were imprints of hands, sometimes positive (the hand dipped into paint and pressed against the wall), sometimes negative (the hand placed against the wall and colour sprayed around it). The peoples of palaeolithic times seemed to have used hands as definitive signs of the human presence and of the human ability to create order in the face of the bewildering chaos of nature.

The hand of man is the mark of man. To lay a hand on is to control, to subject to human dominion. The hand can heal, kill, make and manipulate. It represents the dividing line between man and animal. No wonder that throughout the ages hands have been attributed with magical or miraculous power. The gestures of the hand have symbolic import, perhaps the most striking instance of which is the use of hand-positions or mudras in Hindu ritual dancing which are credited with divine significance and are the identifying signs of either specific deities or certain manifestations of a deity.

It would be wrong to ascribe ritual significance to hand prints found in African mural decoration (60-1/1), but their use is indicative of the extent to which African painting so often reverts to man's most ancient pictorial usage. To peruse its motifs is to experience imagery, the origins of which take us back to the very dawn of art ●

1. The handprint: man's most ancient mark of identity.
2. The chevron pattern shown here reflects the influence of the nearby Zimbabwe Ruins.

DOORS, WINDOWS AND DECORATED INTERIORS

A minute window is almost lost in an expansive field of Sotho floral patterns.

The dark, womb-like interior of the dwelling with its minimal openings to the world is, as it were, the nucleus of life. The interior stands in relation to the world as the embryo does to the macrocosm; the doors and windows are the orifices from the body of the hut to the world. Just as the eyes receive special attention in certain aspects of ritual body painting, so doors and windows are given symbolic or decorative emphasis in mural design.

1. The window from the interior of the hut appears like a moon in a dark sky – on the outside, however, the door is the focal point.
2. A carefully tended plant rests in a deep-set window.

2

1. A Sotho home is protected from the entry of evil spirits by a white barrier around the door frame.
2. A door and window are framed by plants rising from a simulated brick dado. Note the base line of maize plants.

The inordinately small doors that are sometimes encountered are so because when the women of the family, particularly the daughters-in-law, enter the hut, they should not be arrogantly erect and, by stooping, their skirts should modestly cover their legs. (Information received verbally from Malvel Dani.) The smallness of many windows (62-3) is explained by the belief that evil spirts may enter a dwelling, especially at night, through any available opening. In past times, dwellings were windowless, of course, and doorways were sealed for the same reason. The surrounds of doors and windows are often painted white to sanctify the passage to the interior or so that 'good spirits may recognize the entrance at night'. (Information received verbally from V. Gitwa.)

Even when the painted decoration of a dwelling is minimal, doors and occasionally windows are highlighted with colour. Among the Xhosa, the simplest device is a white surround; among the Sotho it is a relief pattern, a raised frame or a

1

2

1 and 2. Designs in light and shade frame windows and doors.

pebble mosaic border (72/1). A frequent metaphor for the window is the flower, leaf or fruit, which may be presented in minimal, geometric terms by a cruciform lozenge (72/1), a diamond (73/2) or some generalized curvilinear design of the type seen in (73/3).

The interiors of huts are sometimes more interesting than the exteriors and may contrast sharply with the bright sunlit external walls. The light from the small windows and the glow of the fires barely illuminate the shapes and forms in the dark, sooty interiors of the Venda home. (In some Southern Sotho homes rooms belonging to parents or parents-in-law may intentionally be made very dark as a reminder that they cannot be freely entered by other members of the family.) As one's eyes adjust to the dark it is possible to make out moulded clay chairs and shelves on which rest blackened pots and

2

Plants grow up the wall as if from seeds in the surrounding
veld. Porcupine quills decorate the foliated entrance.

A jewel-like window in a velvet setting, created by the
additional dimension of clay inlaid with stone.

other kitchen bric-à-brac. In 84-5/1 lithe lines reach up to the
roof as if echoing the sanctity of a small chapel. The delicate
dots are repeated on the moulded shelves.

In contrast to the intimacy of the Venda hut, entering an
Ndebele home is as awe-inspiring as entering a cathedral.
The cool and clean interiors are uncluttered, with sleeping
mats generally rolled in the rafters. Floors are spotless as
much of the ritual of tribal life has to do with hygiene; for example, ammonia in manure, which is one of the ingredients
used in the thin slip on floors, is used as a disinfectant. The
porous qualities of manure render it light, workable and more
durable than dried clay on its own. The cellulose encourages
cohesion and helps to create a strong, hard surface which
can be polished. These floors are a delicate tracery of greys
and beige against which the walls rise in a celebration of brilliant colour like stained-glass windows.

Perhaps influenced by the design of old Welsh dressers

1. A diamond-shaped window is decoratively integrated by repeating its shape in the flanking cruciform plants.
2. As the eye receives special attention in body painting, so does the window in architecture.

Grandeur through humble means: a stencilled design imitating
a wall-paper pattern, and a clay kitchen dresser of striking scale.

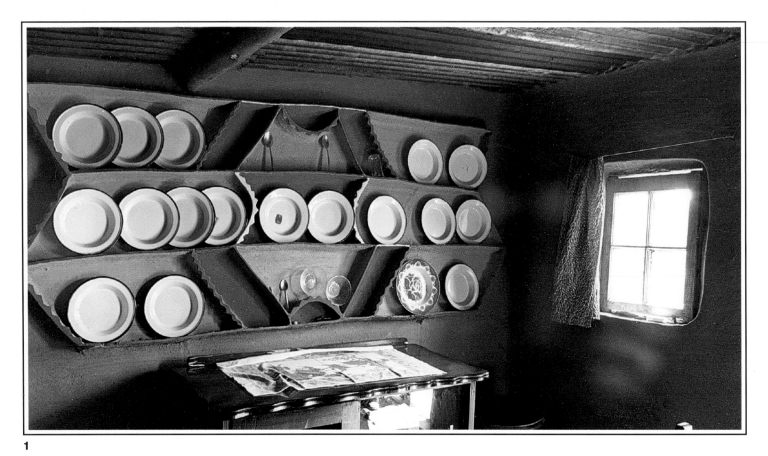

1

1. Dressers are carefully constructed to accommodate
ordinary kitchen utensils with optimum decorative effect.
2. A band of stencilled frieze.

2

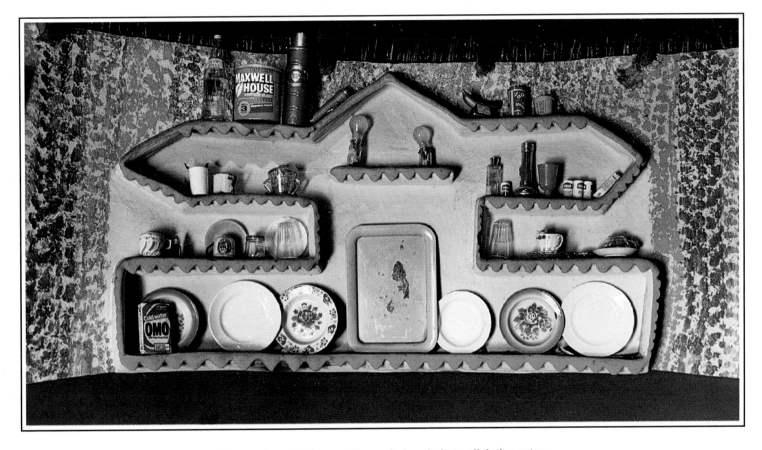

The patterned edges of these shelves imitate oilcloth pantry
liners, and the walls have vertical drops of painted 'wallpaper'.

(76-81) and of oilcloth pantry liners, Sotho women have
produced a type of shelf which is uniquely their own. Moulded from clay, these shelves project from the walls in an end-
less variety of shapes and colours. They fit into the decorative
scheme of the rooms, contrasting with or picking up colours
used on the walls. Often walls are painted in designs which
have been inspired by wallpaper patterns (77); their charm,
however, lies in their free interpretation.

These shelves may be simple shapes in brown or ochre or
highly ornate cut-outs in clay and cardboard. The scalloped

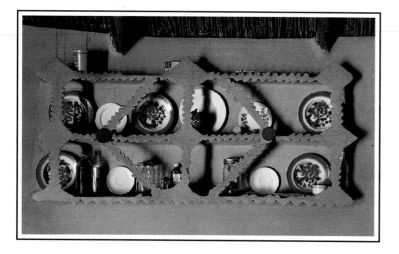

Clay kitchen units are frequently inspired by the forms of old Welsh dressers, catering to man's insatiable desire to display his wealth.

edges, whether standing up or hanging down from the ledges, may have thick cardboard cut-outs set into the clay to provide rigidity and strength. Generally the clay is rolled out like dough, then the patterned edges are cut out, shaped and painted to imitate the appearance of old-fashioned oilcloth pantry liners with decorative borders which were so popular at one time. Sometimes the edgings incorporate paper doilies or parts of egg boxes. An incredible variety of useful and useless objects is arranged on the shelves: washing soaps or coffee, glass baubles, cups and saucers, books and bottles, old torch batteries, and, in homes without electricity, even light bulbs are displayed ●

1

1. Typical of Ndebele mural art, a preoccupation with gables and arches is reflected in this wall unit.
2. The design of this dresser has been influenced by the shapes of ceremonial masks. The colour of the enamelware has dictated the choice of background.

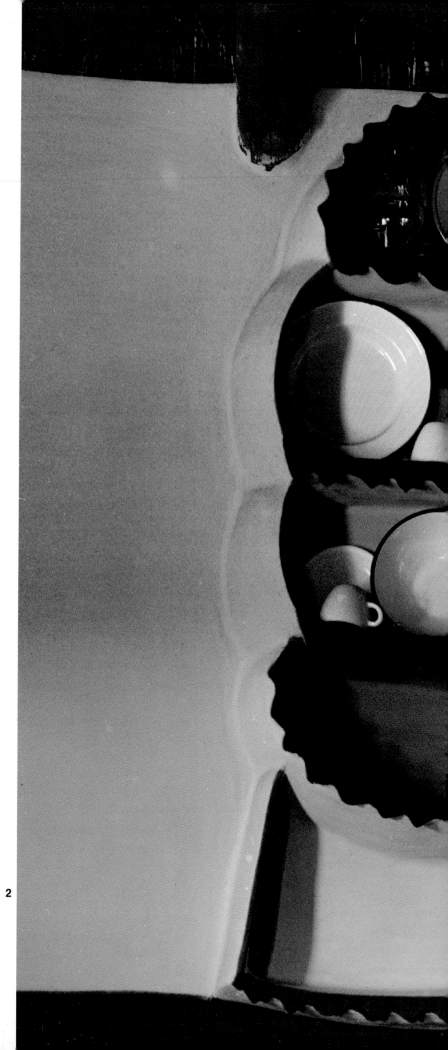

2

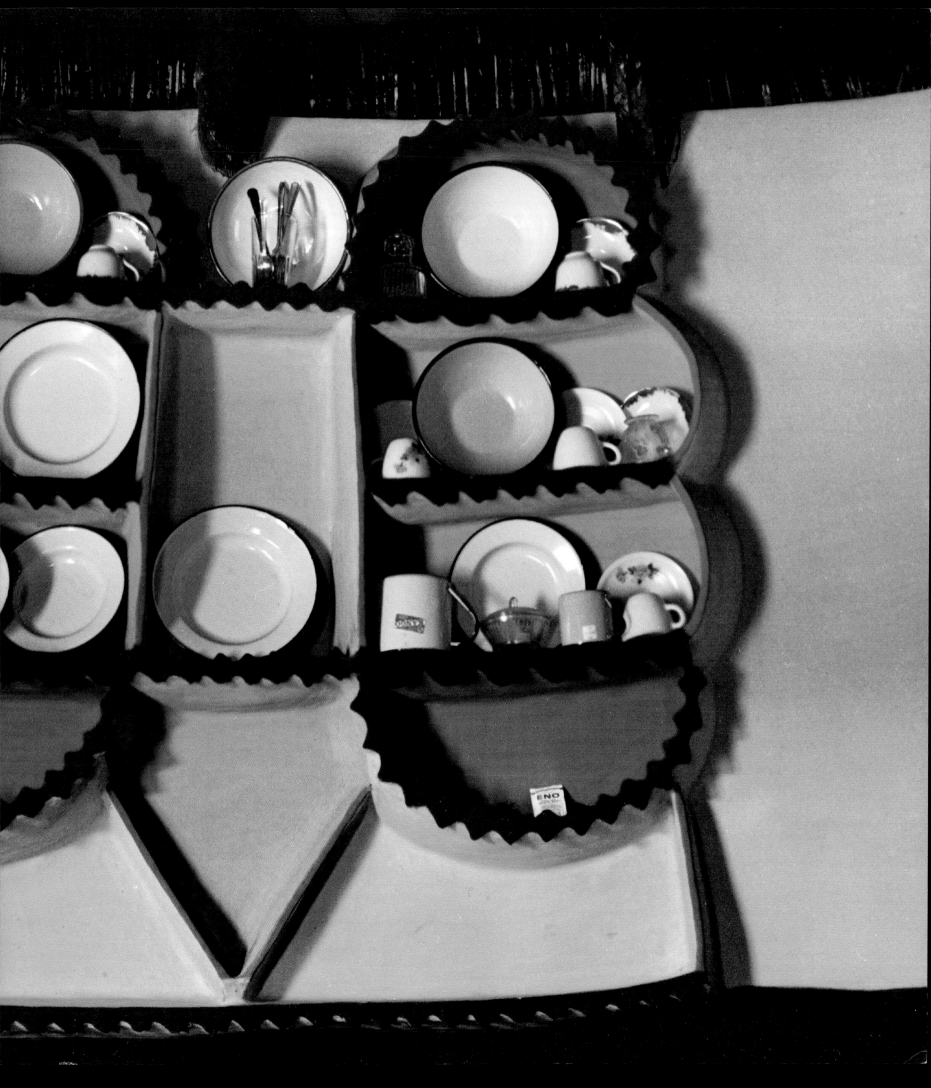

Previous spread: A classical Ndebele interior complete with pediment design, ketting pattern and architectural motifs.

1. A dark 'Gothic' interior with a pointed, interlined arcade and an 'altar piece' of kitchen shelves. Dim light from the tiny window enhances the aura of the room as an inner sanctum.

2. A typical example of fingered floor patterns surrounding a courtyard cooking area.

2

In Ndebele painting the ketting pattern
of the cornice often sets the theme.

NDEBELE MURAL PAINTING

Patterns on commercially produced blankets have influenced the geometric forms of Ndebele wall-paintings.

The original basis of Ndebele painting is linear and monochromatic. It entails the use of a limited range of grey, black and white tones (96-7/2, 98).[20]   This monochrome treatment is believed to represent the most archaic aspect of Ndebele art and is referred to as the first phase. The three phases of Ndebele painting developed in chronological succession but are found today in juxtaposition, as elements of a single, unified style (92-3).

Whatever secondary motifs are introduced in Ndebele designs the actual composition is conditioned by the basic skeleton of the monochrome design.[10] One seldom finds an Ndebele dwelling where this monochrome element is entirely absent even if its existence remains only in the method of plastering the floor. In this style the painter is released from considerations of colour and can therefore indulge in a fluid virtuosity of handling based on the subtlest of tonal relationships.

Today the second and third phases are associated exclu-

1. The painter, her palette and canvas.
2. A Ndebele woman using a toothbrush as a painting implement.
3. Detail of a ketting pattern.

sively with polychrome painting. The second phase depicts plants or patterns based on the diverse elements of the mundane environment in a highly stylized fashion: for example, wrought-iron gates, razor blades, numerals and letters. The third phase entails a more realistic translation of modern urban artefact and architecture, with finials, domes, hanging lights and ornamental balustrades.[2]

Later Ndebele painting notwithstanding, the African has

1. The patterns of ceremonial beadwork provide a constant source of inspiration to Ndebele painters.
2 An uncharacteristically informal version of Ndebele design.

2

an eye for the subtlest relationships of colour sensitively attuned to a range of greys, off-whites, ochres and browns. This is evident in the way Africans make a multitude of distinctions between the many hues of cattle, for they differentiate between colours so closely allied that the European eye can make little or no distinction between them.

Origins of First-phase Decoration

In first-phase decoration, a dun grey slip is applied to the wall as a final plastering coat. Lighter and darker tones are applied over this in liquid washes, producing an effect of woven laths sometimes so faint that they are almost indistinguishable from the grey ground. There is strong archaeological evidence to support the belief that the transfer of woven patterns on to clay walls was a practice known to early man.

One of the oldest African wall-making techniques involves the use of interlaced boughs which is in effect a primitive form of weaving. There are many instances in primeval art of the influence of weaving on painting and architecture. Designs that were first developed in wood and grass weaving, then in pottery and basketwork, influenced the decorative forms used on walls, cornices and ceilings. Plaiting, then, is a primal technique from which the various types of weaving develop, and through weaving much ornamentation. The patterns developed from weaving in coarse materials are imitated in paintings, carvings and pottery. (This tendency to copy the forms of manufactured objects in another medium is known as skeuomorphism.) The world's first great stone building,

1

1

2

the necropolis of Zoser at Sakkara, contained a chamber, the faience tiles of which were designed to imitate reed matting.[9] One of the earliest architectural fabrics was wattlework formed by the interlacing of flexible bough and wands daubed with clay.[11] Similar designs are used by the Ndebele on floors.

Usually the façade of the Ndebele dwelling, as well as the exterior of the courtyard wall parallel to the façade, are painted in the chromatic style; the interiors of these walls, as well as the walls of the forecourt and the side walls of the house may be painted in the simpler graphic first-phase style. Also characteristic of Ndebele decoration is an emphasis on the screenlike quality of the wall by the use of a dark border which encloses the wall like a picture in a frame. The splendour of many of the painted interiors, however, is reminiscent of stained-glass cathedral windows. Generally these cool dark interiors are spotlessly clean. When colour is used here it is subordinated to large masses of monochrome, often on the floors.

1. An example of Sotho wall-painting influenced by Ndebele design.
2. First-phase Ndebele design.

The Later Phases

Light and dark – the simplicity of first-phase Ndebele mural design.

Although some of the designs of the Ndebele would seem to have evolved from their beadwork, they have also developed from their long exposure to commercially woven blankets. The flower designs first modified by the weaving process are then transferred according to skeuomorphic considerations so that the technical limitations of weaving are retained in the rectilinear painted motifs.

Ndebele painting can be architectural not only in the sense that it enhances the structure, but also in the sense that it deals with subject matter that is itself architectural. In this it has links with some of the most ancient forms of decoration. Representations of dwellings often cover the main, central area of a wall decoration, with roofs, walls, steps, doors,

lamps, windows and even gardens being alluded to in a brief, cryptographic, severely rectilinear style.

Sometimes these motifs are easily recognizable (91/3); at other times more practice is needed to decipher the signs. In 89/2 for example, the central area depicts several homes in a dwelling complex, together with courtyards, steps and garden elements. Above the actual window in the centre of the wall is a grey triangle representing the roof of a house. Its entrance is the white square below. It is flanked by green and brown courtyard walls and is approached by means of a pathway. Using this as a key to the interpretation, the mural suddenly comes to life in a series of stylized architectural representations ●

Detail of a painted Ndebele gatepost.

Textured work is created by scraping a kitchen
fork through the plaster before it sets.

SOUTHERN SOTHO
MURAL PAINTING

1. The geometry of Sotho architecture is often mirrored in the designs.

2

1

3

2. and 3. This unusual geometric Sotho mural is the result of Ndebele influence.

When a mixing of peoples occurs as so often happens in areas close to large cities, the immigrants tend to adopt the style of the dominant indigenous group, and at the same time are likely to infuse this style with elements alien to it. Something of this nature occurs in the areas adjacent to Lesotho where there is a tendency to use surface relief decoration.

Ndebele influence can be seen in designs spreading across the whole façade of the dwelling. The patterns generally are basic geometric forms: diamonds, semi-circles, and comma motifs. In most instances some kind of three-dimensionality is given to the wall by the use of deeply stippled textures made by pressing the fingertips into wet plaster or by pressing stones into the surface of the wall. Richness of effect is often obtained almost purely in terms of relief, and colour is subordinated to sculptural effect. Doors, windows and colour areas are often enclosed by raised outlines. Patterns in relief made with kitchen forks are said to denote the contours of ploughed fields and are called *litema* (116-7). They are perhaps the primary trade marks of Southern Sotho painting.

Wall-to-wall flower designs and highlighted windows and doors.

They represent the most archaic mode, and, as a cursory glance through this chapter will show, form the basis of the later painted style.

A common feature is monumental plaster engravings which are in effect reliefs in negative, made in monochrome on the dun surface of the plaster. These monochrome designs are based on flower patterns and are formalized in such a way that they can be juxtaposed and interlocked with maximum decorative effect. When placed on the side walls these monochromes have a subtlety and reticence that are in accord with their secondary position in the overall architectural scheme. Their degree of visibility depends on the angle of light so that they vary in subtlety according to the time of day, alternating a positive with a negative effect. Half the pattern is invisible at any given time. This is a frequent feature in African painting, a geometric means, which produces a result

1. Sotho *litema* designs. Artists equate these relief patterns, often incorporating engraved lines made by using an ordinary kitchen fork, with ploughed fields. **2.** A composition, in negative and positive, of circles and rectangles, representing flowers.

2

A window set in a stylized tree produced in Sotho-Ndebele style.

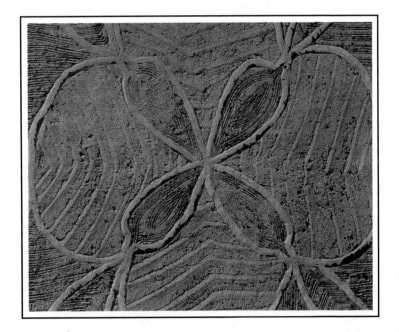

**The simple four-petalled form is
the basis of much Sotho design.**

that is organic and imbued with the movement of nature.

Before special occasions such as engagement parties, weddings, important church celebrations, Easter, or Christmas, an entire village will be redecorated. Sometimes each housewife does her own design. More often the most prestigious craftswoman of the village will be consulted. The redecorating becomes a social event. While the women drink their tea squatting round cleared areas on the ground, the chief 'artist' sketches various schemes in the dust. Once agreement is reached about colours and designs, the women of the village set to work while the 'artist' directs the whole procedure from a central point. If the weather is good, the work will be completed within a week. (Information received verbally from Rosie Mpofu.)

The Sotho housewife takes an enormous pride in her floors and before a special occasion she will apply a film of watered cow or goat dung. While the floor is still wet, she etches a pattern with an ordinary household fork. Friends and neighbours are often called in to approve her work or offer suggestions to improve her design. When the work is complete no one is allowed in the hut or room until the floor is dry. This usually takes about a day, then the village women and chil-

1. Colour and relief, the dual modes of Sotho painting.
2. A four-petalled Sotho design in the *litema* style.

dren sprinkle the floor with water and grind the rough edges with large river pebbles. (Information received verbally from Malvel Dani.)

In some Sotho designs, the tendency for curves to turn back on themselves indicates the presence of an embroyonic spiral and is explained partly by the adoption of flower designs from European fabrics and blanket patterns.

Recent Southern Sotho decoration gives an important place to the written image often as a means of identifying the inhabitants of the dwelling (67/2, 140-1). It may also include the name of the locality or even automobile registration plate numbers.

Mural Art in Lesotho

In Lesotho itself, major emphasis is given to stonework decoration, which tends to take the place of painting. It is in effect a form of elementary mosaic and reflects a reliance on the use of stone in architecture which is far more widespread

A typical Sotho design framed in an Ndebele stepped border – another example of the hybridization of painting styles.

among the Sotho-Tswana group than the Nguni. Stone foundations, dados and kraals are common, and stone decoration is a natural extension of these.

As one would expect, these stone designs are far more rigid and formal than the painted ones; the colouring is more austere, relying on the contrast of stone against stone on clay. They do, however, provide the additional dimension of texture, and, at times, an area of stone and clay will be coated with a single monochrome slip of clay so that the purely textural effect becomes paramount (134-5). Stone decoration has, of course, the benefit of relative permanence. It adds cohesion to the wall, helps protect the clay ground, and is more easily renovated than painted designs.

As the home source of the emigrant modifications of Sotho style and as is typical of home-source designs, these tend to be conservative, even archaic; for instance, the basic four-petalled motif of Lesotho in the emigrant designs becomes far more elaborate and decorative. As always, the design is at

1, 2 and 3. Transcending circles and squares form a variation of deliberate and natural textures.

2

3

one with nature, and the stone mosaics are an expression of the harder, more austere mountain landscape which typifies Lesotho.

Another feature of many dwellings in the region is the use of darker colours around doors and windows and on the lateral extremeties of walls. Coloured areas are often separated by lines raised in relief (130-3). In this type of decoration, painting is typically confined to the corners of the wall and to a cornice running the length of the façade.

The Melting Pot

Although to the north of Lesotho the Sotho people remain numerically dominant, the style of their art is modified by a mixture of primarily Ndebele and other elements, and the region

1

2

1. The scaling of these forms seems like a relic from the Bronze Age, but in reality is due to the demands of available wall space – hence the diminished size of the horses, and the more expansive dimensions of the wagon.
2. A stark pattern of diamonds and triangles gracefully accommodated on a Sotho façade.

2

1

1. Suburban influence causes this break in traditional style.

2. Black and white are used with the same intensity as the primary colours in this compilation of styles typical of the 'melting pot' (see page 118).

has effectively produced a hybrid Sotho-Ndebele style. In 120/2 for example, the concentration of geometricized foliate motifs around door and windows is typically Sotho as is the colour range of the façade, whereas the cornice composed of a chain or 'ketting' of stepped cruciform shapes is a typically Ndebele device.

Several instances are found where this 'ketting' motif is modified to imitate veranda lattice-work, as can be seen at the bottom of the wall in 120/2. The veranda effect may then be strengthened by the inclusion of painted uprights supporting the cornice at the corners of the wall. In this instance the illusion of a projecting veranda is strengthened because the central wall area, which is darker, tends to recede, while the lighter parts project. By such means spatial effects are often incorporated into the seemingly flat, purely two-dimensional designs of African art.

Dwellings may be decorated with jagged diamonds and triangles on zigzags (119/2, 122-3), corresponding with the play of light on the surrounding growth and especially the omnipresent maize-plants, the leaves of which are cut by the light into sharply contrasted triangles of light and dark.

Plates 1, 2 and 3 on pages 124-5 represent an ultimate merging of Ndebele and Sotho styles. The earthy colour range, in black, white, brown, red ochre and sometimes

1

1. A study in varied pattern and
shadow effects. The painted areas
appear to be in full light while the
scraped pattern recedes into
shadow, their design echoed by
the limbs of the children.
2. Decoration expresses the
fertility of women.

2

green is more typically Sotho, as are the decorative motifs on the secondary walls, the intrusion of embryonic spirals and four-petalled flowers, while the bold geometry of the forms, the stepped lozenges, the 'ketting' patterns of the cornices, and the tendency to create overall effects are characteristically Ndebele. These plates also show a widespread tendency in this region to use large areas of brilliantly coloured red oxide set off against black, and to finish the drawing in white outline.

One of the best examples of the hybrid style may be seen on pages 126-7. Here a natural red ochre obtained from a local clay deposit has been combined with shop-bought green distemper, and the combinations of these hues with black and white grace the wall with a brilliantly polychromatic effect.

Another noteworthy feature of the region is the presence of an overt figuration based on animal life, such as a monumental cart with horses (118/1) or the huge wall-length fishes seen in 120-1/1, one of which has an extended tail fin which is also a brilliant blue door. The stylization of the animals here brings to mind the motifs of Celtic or Bronze Age art, while the circular forms of wheels and loaded bales help create an effect as monumental as an Etruscan fresco. The painting of animal themes is far from common in the mural art of southern Africa, and this may well be explained by the woman's traditional role. Her concern is with the plant world, while that of the

1

1, 2 and 3. A merging of Sotho and Ndebele styles: Ndebele in the bold use of geometric elements, Sotho in the early colour scale.

2

animal is the domain of the man.

Travelling from this region towards the borders of KwaZulu, one notices an increasing simplicity of design until eventually the dwellings become quite devoid of painted decoration, without even a frame of whitewash around the doors or windows. Dwellings made of clay gradually give way to structures made exclusively of wood, reeds and grass, which are unsuitable as supports for painting ●

3

Another example of the hybrid Sotho-Ndebele style and a brilliantly chromatic mingling of natural and synthetic colour.

1. A dictionary of African forms.
2. Enormous plant designs lend grandeur to the humble dwellings of the Southern Sotho.

2

1

1. The window – shield or pegged hide?
2. The stippled effect on the walls is created by fingers pressed into damp plaster then set with pebbles.
3. Highly abstract plant motifs frequently surround doors and windows.

1. Cattle dung is used both as a fuel and as an additive to wall plaster.
2. The primary colours of African art – ochre, terracotta and blue.
3. A study in minimalism.

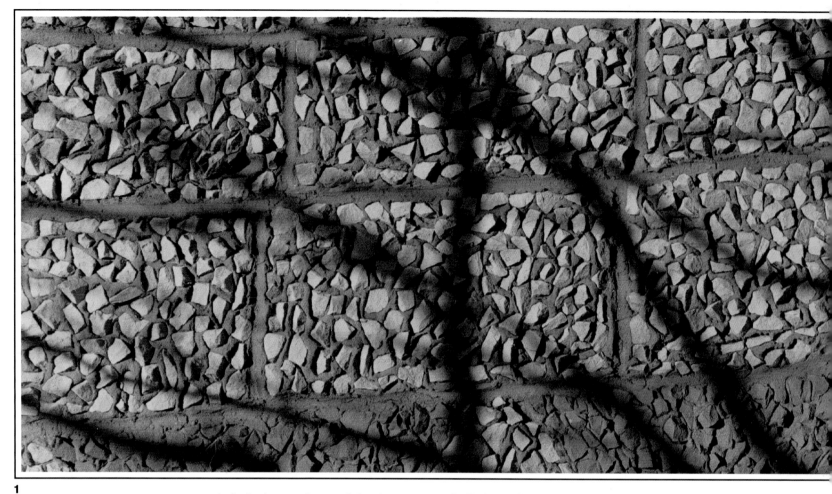

1. A shadow on the rough-hewn geometry of a Sotho wall.
2. Stone designs move across the wall like the shadows of colossal leaves.

3. Readily available stone provides a durable cladding to the dwelling and aptly expresses the harshness of the country.

3

The austerity of Lesotho's landscape is reflected in its mural design.

1

1. A study in harmony – dwelling and landscape.
2. In Lesotho the texture of materials – mud and stone – tends to replace painting.

2

Malvel Dani's freshly painted home, a floral
kaleidoscope of mellow earth shades.

MALVEL DANI

1

1. Shimmering walls reflect the colours of the veld.
2. Malvel Dani.

From the first moment we met Malvel Dani while travelling in the Orange Free State we recognized her as an exceptional woman. Her newly built home was in the final stages of completion and the freshly plastered walls undecorated.

The following year we returned at the end of the summer. Our excitement mounted as we walked through the tall bleached grass and dried flowers. Her home was barely perceptible in the distance and as we approached it slowly came into focus, the walls shimmering in the reflected colours of the veld.

Over the years we returned whenever we happened to be in the area and we were never disappointed. The designs changed as if one was looking through a kaleidoscope –

1. A wall ablaze with flowers, delicately outlined.
2. A side wall showing a more stylized variation of the floral theme.

sometimes bolder and more graphic, sometimes the colours contrasted more strongly, sometimes a central theme with gentle variations, but always harmonious with the surrounding countryside.

For a few years we were unable to visit her but finally decided to make a special effort to see her again. Eagerly we anticipated a new delight, a new example of her outstanding artistry. Imagine our feelings as we stumbled through the veld and looked in vain for her home. We could find nothing. Eventually we made out the familiar peach tree, but that was all. Her home had melted back into the soil from which it had

The African Mural

1

1. and 2.
The same wall dramatically
different a few years later,
a change in mood reflecting
the intervening years of drought.

been created. In a few months the bush would completely cover all traces of its existence.

We are grateful to have met Malvel Dani and so many other artists. We communicated in a combination of African dialects, English, Afrikaans and sign language with much hilarity. They brought us samples of the clay they used and showed us the back walls where they had worked out their designs. We consider it a great privilege to have shared so much. As the farmers build new modern homes for their employees and as so many seek to live nearer to the cities, this work is in danger of extinction. This is our tribute to the little-known mural artists of southern Africa ●

1. The design shifts subtly with the changing roofline.
2. A montage of triangles, circles and squares, bordered by the chevron pattern representing water.

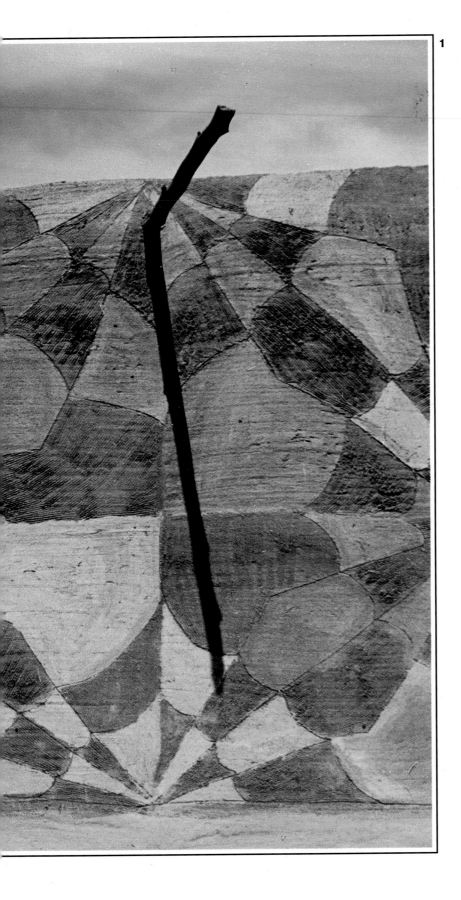

1. A web of shapes reveals an obsession with plant forms.
2. Perhaps marriage brought about this joyous transformation (hence the change in initials). After only one year the earthy colours are rejuvenated with the addition of white.

A side wall showing a more stylized variation of the floral theme.

Born of the soil, grass and trees the
homestead emerges from the flat countryside.

Scorched by the Free State sun, a peach
tree graces the front of Malvel Dani's home.

'And as for man, his days are of grass;
As a flower in the field, so he flourisheth.'

Isiah 40.v.7.

Malvel Dani's palace of mud had melted back into
the soil from which it had risen.

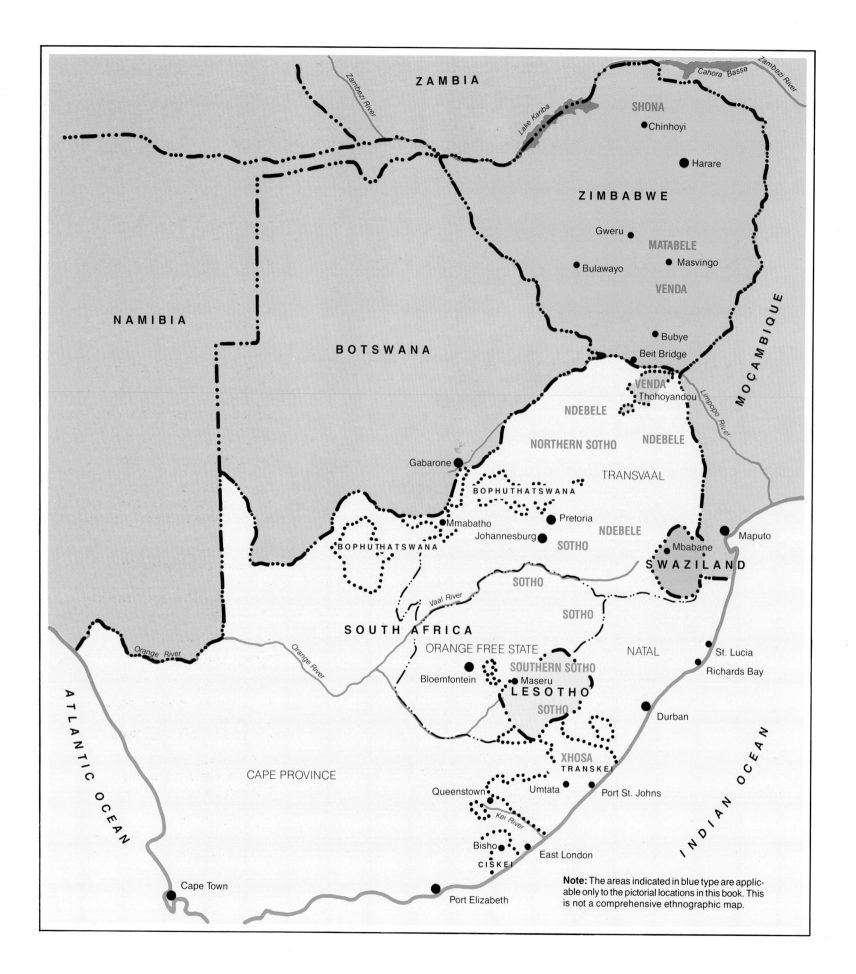

Note: The areas indicated in blue type are applicable only to the pictorial locations in this book. This is not a comprehensive ethnographic map.

PICTORIAL LOCATIONS

The pictorial locations refer to the ethnic group represented by the mural in each photograph, as well as its geographical location.

Half-title page
Sotho, Southern Free State

Title page
Sotho, Southern Transvaal

Pages 4 and 5
Sotho, Southern Transvaal

Page 6
Sotho, north of Lesotho

Pages 8 and 9
Shangaan, Zimbabwean Highveld

Pages 10 and 11
Shona, Chinhoyi, Zimbabwe

Pages 12 and 13
1. Sotho, Southern Free State
2. Sotho, Southern Free State

Pages 14 and 15
Venda, Limpopo Valley, Zimbabwe

Page 16
Shona, Chinhoyi, Zimbabwe

Page 17
Shona, Chinhoyi, Zimbabwe

Pages 18 and 19
1. Sotho, Southern Transvaal
2. Sotho, Southern Transvaal

Pages 20 and 21
Ndebele, Central Transvaal

Pages 22 and 23
1. Xhosa, Umtata district, Transkei
2. Ndebele, Central Transvaal

Pages 24 and 25
1. Sotho, Lesotho
2. Ndebele, Eastern Transvaal

Pages 26 and 27
Sotho, Lesotho

Pages 28 and 29
Ndebele, North-eastern Transvaal

Page 31
Ndebele, North-eastern Transvaal

Pages 32 and 33
Ndebele, Central Transvaal

Pages 34 and 35
1. Ndebele, Central Transvaal
2. Sotho, Lesotho

Pages 36 and 37
1. Sotho, Lesotho
2. Sotho, Lesotho

Pages 38 and 39
1. Ndebele, North-eastern Transvaal
2. Ndebele, North-eastern Transvaal

Pages 40 and 41
Venda, Bubye district, Southern Zimbabwe

Pages 42 and 43
1. Venda, Bubye district, Southern Zimbabwe
2. Venda, Bubye district, Southern Zimbabwe

Pages 44 and 45
Shangaan, Zimbabwean Lowveld

Pages 46 and 47
Shangaan, Zimbabwean Lowveld

Pages 48 and 49
1. Shona, Zimbabwean Highveld

2. Shangaan, Zimbabwean Lowveld

Pages 50 and 51
Sotho, North-eastern Free State

Pages 52 and 53
1. Sotho, Southern Transvaal
2. Sotho, Southern Transvaal

Pages 54 and 55
Shona, Chinhoyi district, Zimbabwe

Page 56
Shona, Chinhoyi district, Zimbabwe

Page 57
Sotho, Southern Transvaal

Pages 58 and 59
1. Xhosa, North-eastern Transkei
2. Xhosa, North-eastern Transkei

Pages 60 and 61
1. Shona, Chinhoyi district, Zimbabwe
2. Matabele, Masvingo district, Zimbabwe

Pages 62 and 63
Sotho, Lebowa district

Pages 64 and 65
1. Shangaan, Mwenezi district, Zimbabwe
2. Sotho, Eastern Free State

Pages 66 and 67
1. Sotho, Eastern Free State
2. Sotho, Lesotho

Pages 68 and 69
1. Sotho, Eastern Free State
2. Xhosa, North-eastern Transkei

Pages 70 and 71
Sotho, Central Transvaal

Page 72
Sotho, Lesotho

Page 73
1. Ndebele, Northern Transvaal
2. Sotho, Lesotho

Pages 74 and 75
Ndebele, Eastern Transvaal

Page 76
Ndebele, Eastern Transvaal

Page 77
Ndebele, Eastern Transvaal

Pages 78 and 79
Ndebele, Eastern Transvaal

Pages 80 and 81
1. Ndebele, Eastern Transvaal
2. Ndebele, Eastern Transvaal

Pages 82 and 83
Ndebele, Eastern Transvaal

Pages 84 and 85
1. Shangaan, Mwenezi district, Zimbabwe
2. Shangaan, Quagga Pan, Zimbabwe

Pages 86 and 87
Ndebele, Central Transvaal

Page 88
Ndebele, Central Transvaal

Page 89
Ndebele, Central Transvaal

Pages 90 and 91
1. Ndebele, Central Transvaal
2. Ndebele, Central Transvaal
3. Ndebele, Central Transvaal

Pages 92 and 93
Ndebele, North-eastern Transvaal

Page 94
Ndebele, North-eastern Transvaal

Page 95
Ndebele, Eastern Free State

Pages 96 and 97
1. Sotho, Southern Transvaal
2. Ndebele, Central Transvaal

Page 98
Ndebele, Eastern Transvaal

Page 99
Ndebele, Eastern Transvaal

Pages 100 and 101
Sotho, North-eastern Free State

Pages 102 and 103
Sotho, North-eastern Free State

Pages 104 and 105
Sotho, Eastern Free State

Pages 106 and 107
1. Sotho, Southern Transvaal
2. Sotho, Central Free State

Pages 108 and 109
Sotho, Eastern Free State

Page 110
Sotho, Eastern Free State

Page 111
Sotho, Eastern Free State

Pages 112 and 113
1. Sotho, Eastern Free State
2. Sotho, Lesotho

Pages 114 and 115
Sotho, North-eastern Free State

Pages 116 and 117
1. Sotho, Eastern Free State
2. Sotho, Eastern Free State
3. Sotho, Eastern Free State

Pages 118 and 119
1. Sotho, Transvaal/Orange Free State border
2. Sotho, Transvaal/Orange Free State border

Pages 120 and 121
1. Sotho, Southern Transvaal
2. Sotho/Ndebele, North-eastern Transvaal

Pages 122 and 123
1. Sotho, South-eastern Transvaal
2. Sotho, Northern Free State

Pages 124 and 125
1. Sotho, Nothern Free State
2. Sotho, Northern Free State
3. Sotho, Northern Free State

Pages 126 and 127
Sotho/Ndebele, North-eastern Transvaal

Pages 128 and 129
Sotho, Eastern Free State

Pages 130 and 131
Sotho, Lesotho

Pages 132 and 133
1. Sotho, Lesotho
2. Sotho, Lesotho
3. Sotho, Lesotho

Pages 134 and 135
1. Sotho, Lesotho
2. Sotho, Lesotho
3. Sotho, Lesotho

Pages 136 and 137
Sotho, Lesotho

Pages 138 and 139
1. Sotho, Lesotho
2. Sotho, Lesotho

Pages 140 to 159
Sotho, Eastern Free State

GLOSSARY

architrave	moulding around a doorway or window opening
corbel	a bracket, usually of stone or brick
crennellations	any teeth or notches of a parapet-like structure
dado	lower part of interior wall decorated differently from upper part
emnyango	house entrance
esangweni	courtyard entrance
faience	tin-glazed earthenware
finials	ornament at the top of spire or gable
isikwens	chevron patterns
lath	thin, narrow strip of wood used as framework to support tiles or plaster
litema	patterns made with kitchen fork that denote the contours of ploughed fields
pilaster	a shallow rectangular column attached to the face of a wall
pointillism	dots of unmixed colour juxtaposed on a white ground so that they fuse in the viewer's eye
skeuomorphism	tendancy to copy forms of manufactured objects in another medium
slip	clay mixed with water to a creamy constituency
tracery	pattern of interlacing ribs
udaka	mud

BIBLIOGRAPHY

1. Balfour, H. *The Evolution of Decorative Art*, London, Percival, 1983.

2. Berman, E. *Art and Artists of South Africa*, Cape Town, Balkema, 1970.

3. Boas, F. *Primitive Art*, New York, Dover, 1955.

4. Broster, J. *Red Blanket Valley*, Johannnesburg, Keartland, 1967.

5. Davidson, B. *Africa: History of a Continent*, London, Weidenfeld and Nicholson, 1966.

6. Frobenius, L. *Madsimu Dsangara*, Graz, Akademische Druk-u Verlaganstalt, 1962.

7. Gerbrands, A.A. *Art as an Element of Culture, Especially in Negro Africa*, Leiden, Brill, 1957.

8. Giedion, S. *The Eternal Present: The Beginnings of Art* (Vol. 1), London, Oxford University Press, 1962.

9. Giedion, S. *The Eternal Present: The Beginnings of Architecture* (Vol. 2), London, Oxford University Press, 1962.

10. Grossert, J., Batiss, W. and Franz, W. *The Art of Africa* Pietermaritzburg, Shuter and Shooter, 1958.

11. Haddon, A.C. *Evolution in Art*, London, Walter Scott, 1895.

12. Huxley, A.J. 'Mandrake' in *Man, Myth and Magic*, London, B.P.C., 1970.

13. Krige, E.J. and J.D. *The Realm of the Rain Queen*, London, Oxford University Press, 1943.

14. Leiris, M. and Delange, J. *African Art*, London, Weidenfeld and Nicholson, 1968.

15. Levi-Straus, C. *Structural Anthropology*, London, Allen Lane, 1968.

16. Marquard, L. and Standing, T. *The Southern Bantu*, London, Oxford University Press, 1939.

17. McKay, J. *The Origin of the Xhosas and Others*, Cape Town, Juta, 1911.

18. Posener, G. *Dictionary of Egyptian Civilization*, London, Methuen, 1962.

19. Sharpe, E. 'Fertility' in *Man, Myth and Magic*, London, B.P.C., 1970.

20. Walton, J. 'Mural Art of the Bantu' in *S.A. Panorama*, April 1965.

21. Weyl, H. in Giedion, S. *The Eternal Present: The Beginnings of Architecture* (Vol.2), London, Oxford University Press, 1962.

INDEX

Page numbers in **bold** type indicate that the subject is illustrated and/or is mentioned in the caption on that page.

A

Abstraction 45
Akkad 56
Ant heap 29–30
Architecture 21, 30, 34, 35
Architrave 163
Art **5,** 13, 17, 19, 30

B

Beadwork **95,** 98
Benin (*see* Dahomey)
Blankets **88,** 98, 112
Blood, ox 29–30
Brick, sun-dried 25, 29
Bronze Age **118,** 124
Bubye (district, Zimbabwe) 161
Bushmen 30, **42,** 47

C

Campbell, John 17
Cave **35**
Chephren 38
Chinhoyi 161
Colours 11, 30, **47, 51,** 95, **112,** 116, 118, 121, **121,** 123, **127, 133,** 142, **142, 151**
Construction 27–30
Corbel 23, 163
Crenellations **25,** 163

D

Dado 52, 116, 163
Dahomey 47
Dani, Malvel 67, 112, **140,** 142, **142,** 147, **157, 159**
Darkness **36,** 38, 68, **68, 85, 98,** 121, **122**
Doors 34, **36, 51,** 65, **65,** 67, **67, 68,** 98, 103, 104, 118, **130**
Dressers 72, **75, 76, 78, 80**

E

Egypt 34, 38, 47, 48, 52, 56, 56, 58
emnyango 38, 163
Engaruka (Tanzania) 23
esangweni 38, 163
Europe, Iron Age 17
Ezana (King) 23

F

Faience 97, 163
Fanagalo 30
Fertility symbols **9,** 42, 47, 48, 52, **122**
Fingo 30
Finial 38, 163
Floors 29, 72, **85,** 97, 111-2

G

Geometric form **2,** 19, **19, 29,** 35, 45, 47, 48, 56, 58, 68, **88, 102,** 103, **103,** 107, 124, **134**
Ghoya 23
Gitwa, V. 67
Guardian figure **38,** 43

H

Hausa 28
Hut 13, 23, 34, 38, 42
Hindu dancing 61

I

Indians,
    Brazilian 19
    British Guianan 19
    Californian 17, 19
    North American 17
Interiors 65, 68, 68, 72, **83, 85, 89,** 97

K

Kabones 23
Kaditshwêne (*see* Kurreechane)

Keyhole entrance **35**
Kurreechane 17
KwaZulu 125

L

Laths 163
Lebowa (district) 161
Lesotho 23, **27,** 103, 112, 116, 118, **137, 139,** 161, 162
Light **19,** 38, 68, **68, 85, 89, 98,** 121, **122**
Limpopo Valley 161
litema 30, 103, **107, 112,** 163
Lobedu 43

M

Magdalenian hunters 38
Mandrake 47
Masvingo (district) 161
Matabele 161
Materials 30, **91, 101**
Mattioli, Pietro Andrea 47
Meriotes 23
Mesopotamia 56, 58
Middle East 17
Moffat, Robert 23
Motifs,
    animals 17, 19, **118,** 123-4, 125
    chevron 52, **55,** 56, **61, 149**
    dot **9,** 47, 48, 52, 72
    flower **6, 11, 13,** 19, 35, 58, **63, 104,** 107, **107,** 112, **140, 145, 153**
    hands 61, **61**
    isikwens 52, **52,** 163
    ketting **13, 83, 86, 91,** 121, 123
    leaf 35
    mound 6, 45, 58
    mountainous terrain 53, **55,** 56
    plant **17,** 19, 34, **40,** 41, 42, **42, 45,** 47, 48, **48, 58,** 65, **67, 71, 73, 128, 130, 151**
    seed **17, 71**
    sexual symbols 47
    step **2, 19,** 56, **58, 114**

tree 29, 56, 58, **108**
vase **42, 45,** 47, **47**
water 52, **55,** 56, **149**
Mpofu, Rosie 111
Mud 28, 29
Music **4,** 45
Mwenezi (district) 161, 162

N

Nature, man's relationship with **2,** 29, **40,** 45, 47, 56
Ndebele 19, **25, 29,** 30, 30, **33,** 34, 35, 38, 43, 47, 52, 56, 72, **80, 83, 86,** 88, **88, 89, 91, 92, 95,** 97, **99,** 103, 118, 121, 123, 161, 162
first phase **21, 35,** 88, 95, 97, **97, 98**
Ndebele-Sotho (mixed styles) **97,** 108, 114, 121, **124, 127,** 162
second phase 88, 91
third phase 88, 91
Near East 58
Nguni 25, 42, 52, 116
Nigeria 28
Nobatian towns 23

O

Orange Free State 142, **157**
border with Transvaal 162
Eastern 161, 162
North-eastern 161, 162
Northern 23, 162
Southern 161

P

Pantry liners 77, **77,** 78
Phoenicia 56, 58
Pilaster 24, 163
Pointillism 163
Pottery 56, 95

Q

Qebe 34

Quagga Pan 162

R

Ritual 42-3, 45, 72
Roof structure **22,** 27

S

Sakkara 38, 97
Scandinavia 56
Sculpture, African 17
Shangaan 161, 162
Shelves 68, 77, **77,** 85
Shona 11, 161
Skeuomorphism 95, 98, 163
Slip 95, 163
Sotho **2, 13,** 17, 30, 30, 42, 56, **63,** 67, **67,** 77, **102, 103,** 111, **111, 112,** 116, 118, **118,** 121, 123, **134,** 161, 162
Sotho-Ndebele (mixed styles) **97, 108, 114,** 121, **124, 127,** 162
Southern **6,** 29, 68, 103, 112, **128**
Sotho-Tswana (group) 116
Space-transition **30**
Stencil, use of 30, **75, 76**
Stone, use of 23, **25, 72,** 112, 116, 118, **134, 135, 139**
Sumeria 56
Symmetry 35-6
bilateral 35, 36, 38
rotational 36, 38
shifting 36

T

Taung 23
Techniques **6,** 30
Tools **6,** 30, **100,** 103, **107**
Tracery 72, 163
Transkei 34, 58, 161
North-eastern 161
Transvaal
border with Orange Free State 162
Central 161, 162
Eastern 161, 162

North-eastern 161, 162
Northern 162
Southern 23
Two-dimensionality 38, 58

U

udaka 28, 163
Umtata (district) 161

V

Venda **14,** 23, 68, 72

W

Wallpaper **75,** 77, **77**
Wattle and daub 25, 27
Weaving 17, 28, 95, 98
Windows **13, 27,** 34, 58, **63,** 65, **65,** 67, **67,** 68, **68, 72, 73, 85,** 98, **103, 104,** 118, **130**
Women, role of **2,** 13, **17,** 29, 30, 41, 47, 48, 52, 67, **91, 122,** 124

X

Xhosa **22,** 30, 52, **58,** 67, 161

Z

Zeerust 17
Zimbabwe **11, 14,** 56, 161, 162
Highveld 161
Lowveld 161
Ruins 23, **61**
Southern 161
Zoser (necropolis of) 38, 97